Contents

...fessional Publishing

an imprint of Reed Educational & Professional Publishing,
Chicago, Illinois

Customer Service 888-454-2279
Visit our website at www.heinemannlibrary.com

Designed by Depke Design
Printed and bound at Lake Book Manufacturing

06 05 04 03 02
10 9 8 7 6 5 4 3 2 1

Library of Congress Cataloging-in-Publication Data
Ansary, Mir Tamim.
  Earth day / Mir Tamim Ansary.
      p. cm. -- (Holiday histories)
Includes bibliographical references and index.
  ISBN 1-58810-220-3
  1. Earth Day--Juvenile literature. 2. Environmentalism--Juvenile
literature. 3. Environmental protection--Juvenile literature. [1. Earth
Day. 2. Environmental protection. 3. Holidays.] I. Title.
  GE195.5 .A57 2001
  333.7--dc21
                                        2001000070

Acknowledgments
The author and publishers are grateful to the following for permission to reproduce copyright material:
Cover photograph: AP/Wide World
pp. 4–5 Guy Palm; pp. 5B, 7, 19, 21, 23 Corbis; p. 6 Underwood Photo Archives; p. 8 North Wind Pictures; p. 9 The Granger Collection; pp. 10, 16 Spencer Grant/Photo Edit; p. 11 Jeff Greenberg/Photo Edit; pp. 12, 13 Alan Oddie/ Photo Edit; p. 14 Tony Freeman/Photo Edit; p. 15 Mark Richard/Photo Edit; pp. 17, 26 A Ramey/Photo Edit; p. 18 John Elk III/Bruce Coleman, Inc.; p. 20 AP/Wide World; p. 22 SuperStock; p. 24 David Young-Wolff/Photo Edit; p. 25 Tony Stone/Getty; p. 27 David Barber/Photo Edit; p. 28 Steve L. Hilty/Bruce Coleman, Inc.; p. 29 Image Bank/Getty.

Some words are shown in bold, **like this.** You can find
out what they mean by looking in the glossary.

Earth Day

Mir Tamim Ansary

Heinemann Library
Chicago, Illinois

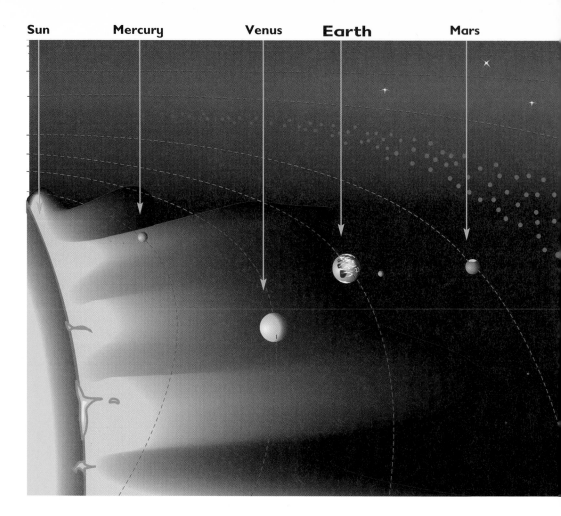

Sun   Mercury   Venus   **Earth**   Mars

Our Home Planet

Nine planets circle around our sun.
Each one is a ball of **matter** moving
through space. And the third one is
our home planet, Earth.

Jupiter Saturn Uranus Neptune Pluto

April 22 is known as Earth Day. This
is a day to celebrate our planet. It is
a day to think about its problems, too.

Before There Was Earth Day

When your grandparents were born, there was no such thing as Earth Day. Back then, few people worried about Earth.

Most people thought they could never harm our planet. They thought our planet was too big to be harmed. People thought this for a long time.

More and More People

Thousands of years ago, there were not many people on Earth. They lived in tiny villages. The rest of the world was **wilderness.**

Over time, Earth's **population** kept growing. People spread to most continents. More and more towns formed. Some towns became huge, crowded cities.

Machines Change Life

The growing **population** needed more and more food. In fact, people needed or wanted more **goods** of every kind. They invented machines to make goods faster.

To make more goods, people had to use more **resources.** They cut down more trees and dug up more metals. They used more of everything Earth provides.

The Pollution Problem

Fuels, such as **coal** and oil, made the new machines work. These fuels make harmful **wastes** as they burn. Such waste in the air is called air **pollution.**

The new machines created water pollution, too. Harmful wastes came out of factories, farms, and even homes. Pollution poured into streams, rivers, and lakes.

The Trash Problem

The more **goods** people used, the more trash they created. Getting rid of this trash became another problem. **Dumps** were filling up fast.

Nuclear power plants give off steam that you can see, but they also make dangerous wastes that you cannot see.

Nuclear power plants make electricity. They also make dangerous **wastes.** These wastes must be stored very carefully in special places.

Trouble for Animals

*People are building their homes in **wilderness** places, harming the plants and animals around them.*

Humans began changing Earth to fit their needs. They drained swamps, cut down jungles, and dammed rivers. They changed the places where animals lived.

A habitat is the place where an animal lives. Many animals had trouble surviving once their habitats were gone. Some even became **extinct.**

Giant pandas are running out of habitat. They are in danger of dying out.

Worrying About Earth

Yellowstone became our first national park in 1872.

In our country, some lands were made into parks. People were not allowed to live in these places or destroy them. But other places kept getting **polluted.**

In 1969, a river in Ohio got so polluted, it caught fire! By this time, many people knew the **environment** was in trouble. These people were worried.

Oil on the polluted Cuyahoga River in Ohio caught fire on June 22, 1969. Some flames were as high as a five story building!

Earth Day Is Born

A man from Wisconsin, Gaylord Nelson, came up with the idea for Earth Day. He said there should be a special day to **honor** Earth. On April 22, 1970, the first Earth Day was celebrated.

Gaylord Nelson

That day, about twenty million people
around the country took part in Earth Day
activities. They showed their concern for
Earth. For example, they marched and
gave speeches about how to help Earth.

Laws to Help Earth

Within two years of 1970, two new laws were passed. These laws made it harder for people to **pollute** air and water. Now, some polluted places are being cleaned up.

Another important law was passed in 1973. It protects animals that are in danger of becoming **extinct.** It keeps their habitats from being destroyed.

Laws now protect animals near extinction, like these bald eagles.

People Helping Earth

Some people are now helping Earth by **recycling.** They recycle glass, metal, paper, and other materials. Recycling helps save **resources.** It also creates less trash.

Cars make a lot of air **pollution.** Some people are trying to use cars less often. They get around on bicycles and public buses when they can.

Science to the Rescue

Scientists are working on inventions to help Earth. An electric car is one such invention. It does not create air **pollution** as it runs.

*These windmills make electricity without making harmful **wastes**.*

Today, electricity can be made from the sun and the wind. Someday, wind and sunlight may replace **coal** and oil as **fuels**. Scientists are working on these ideas, too.

Our Planet's Future

What will our planet be like in the future? Green and clean? Or gray and **polluted?** That depends on us.

Our actions will make the difference.
Earth Day is a good time to think about
the **environment.** What role will you play
in the story of Planet Earth?

Important Dates

Earth Day

1824	The first **fuel-**burning engine is invented
1850	London, England becomes the first city with one million people
1872	Yellowstone becomes the world's first national park
1897	The United States National Forest system begins
1903	Pelican Island becomes the first safe place set aside for animals in the United States
1962	Rachel Carson's book, *Silent Spring*, warns people that the **environment** is in big trouble
1970	The first Earth Day is celebrated
1970	The Clean Air Act is signed into law
1972	The Clean Water Act is signed into law
1973	The **Endangered** Species Act is passed to help endangered animals
1989	The *Exxon Valdez* oil tanker spills eleven million gallons of oil in the waters near Alaska
1994	The bald eagle comes off the list of endangered animals

★

Glossary

coal black matter that is dug from the ground and used for fuel

dump big hole in the ground where trash is buried

endangered group of plants or animals that are in danger of dying out because there are so few

environment world that surrounds us and affects how we live

extinct group of plants or animals that have died out and can never live again

fuel something that is burned to create energy

goods things people use

honor to show respect for someone or something

matter what things are made up of

pollution trash or noise that spoils a place and can hurt animals; to create pollution is to pollute

population number of people in a place

recycling using an item or material over again

resources useful things found in or on Earth

waste unwanted material left over after something is made or burned

wilderness area not touched or changed by people

More Books to Read

Morichon, David. *Pollution? No Problem!* Brookfield, Conn.: Millbrook Press, 1998.

Penny, Malcolm. *Talking About Our Environment.* Austin, Tex.: Raintree Steck-Vaughn, 2000.

Royston, Angela. *Recycling.* Austin, Tex.: Raintree Steck-Vaughn, 1998.

Index